D1232034

ARMY
AND
NAVY
FOOTBALL

BY K.C. KELLEY

The
**Child's
World**®
childsworld.com

Published by The Child's World®
1980 Lookout Drive • Mankato, MN 56003-1705
800-599-READ • www.childsworld.com

Cover: Andy Lewis/AP Images.
Interior: AP Images: Cal Sport Media 4; 9; Jacqueline
Larma 14; 17 top; Newscom: Derek Hamilton/
UPI 10; Gavin Baker/Icon Sportswire 12 top; Andy
Lewis/Icon Sportswire 12 bottom; Frank DeBrando/
Icon SMI 17 bottom; Danie Kucin Jr./Icon Sportswire
18; Kostas Lymperopoulos/Cal Sport Media 21.

ISBN 9781503850347 (Reinforced Library Binding)
ISBN 9781503850590 (Portable Document Format)
ISBN 9781503851351 (Online Multi-user eBook)
LCCN: 2021930284

Printed in the United States of America

*A sailor and a player, Navy
quarterback Malcolm Perry
looks for room to run.*

CONTENTS

Why We Love College Football   4

WHY WE LOVE COLLEGE FOOTBALL

College football fans fill stadiums each fall. Pennants wave. Bands play and fans sing fight songs! The sport is one of America's most popular. Millions of people follow their favorite teams. They wear school colors and hope for big wins.

Veterans Stadium in Philadelphia was packed every year for the Army-Navy football game.

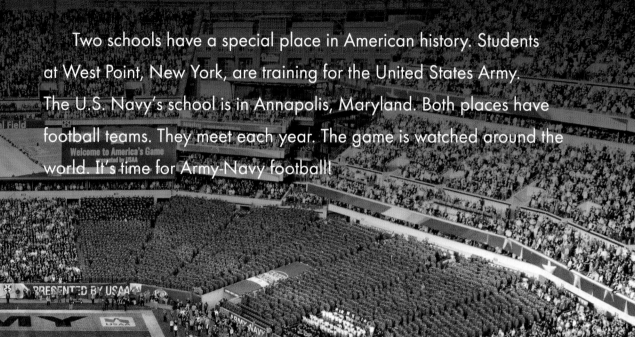

Two schools have a special place in American history. Students at West Point, New York, are training for the United States Army. The U.S. Navy's school is in Annapolis, Maryland. Both places have football teams. They meet each year. The game is watched around the world. It's time for Army-Navy football!

Above: The 1890 Navy team did not wear those striped caps during their games!

Right: Future president Dwight Eisenhower

Below: The letters on these 1891 team shirts stand for United States Military Academy.

Early Days

Navy students are called Midshipmen. In 1879, some "Middies" tried to start a football team. School leaders said no. They thought the game was too rough! In 1882, Navy officially started playing the sport. Navy's teams had **winning records** from 1904 through 1923.

Army's first team played in 1890. The Cadets' first game was against Navy. The

> ## PRESIDENT FOOTBALL
>
> Dwight D. Eisenhower played for Army in 1911 and 1912. He was a running back. As an Army general, he led American forces in World War II (1941–45). He was later president of the United States from 1953–1961.

Midshipmen won the first game between the teams. Army won the second. A famous **rivalry** was born!

Army football had its first perfect season in 1914. It repeated at 9-0 in 1916. Army's best years were ahead of them, however.

CHAPTER TWO

Glory Years: Army

Members of the U.S. Army helped win World War II (1939–45). Army football teams won three national titles at the same time (1944, 1945, and 1946). Army used a powerful running attack.

A 1946 game against Notre Dame was one of the most famous in college football history. The teams were ranked No. 1 and No. 2. The game ended in a 0–0 tie!

Army did not have many great seasons in the next few **decades**. However, the Black Knights have played well recently. The team played in four **bowl games** from 2016 through 2020.

In 1945, Army hero Felix "Doc" Blanchard (35) shows off his moves in a win over Michigan! ➤

CHAPTER THREE

Glory Years: Navy

The first great Navy team played in 1926. They won 9 games and tied 1. They earned a national championship.

Navy football has been strong in the 2000s. They played in 15 bowl games from 2003 to 2019. The 2019 team was one of the country's best. Navy tied a school record with 11 wins. A win in the Liberty Bowl **capped off** a great season. Malcolm Perry ran for 2,017 yards. That's the most ever by a college quarterback! More importantly, Navy beat Army 14 seasons in a row (2002–2015)!

WAY OUT WEST

The Army-Navy game has only been played in the West once. The 1983 game was held in the Rose Bowl in Pasadena, California. The game raised money for military charities. Navy won 42–13.

◄ *Malcolm Perry was at Navy training for a career at sea. On the football team, he did most of his work running on the ground!*

CHAPTER FOUR
4

Army Traditions

Soldiers are used to marching. Army cadets are no different. The entire student body marches onto the field before the Army-Navy game. Their gray capes are a thrilling sight for fans. The cadets then fill one side of the stadium. And they stand up for the entire game!

Army's **mascot** is a mule. The animals have long been a part of the Army. They carried gear into battle. At each game, an Army mule is on the sidelines.

Army soldiers parachute into the stadium before each game. They deliver a game ball to the field.

The school's most important tradition is the cadets' loud cheer: "Beat Navy!"

**Above: Here comes the game ball!
Army parachute teams land on the
field before each game.**

**Left: One of Army's team nicknames
is The Black Knights of the Hudson.
Here's a student wearing the Black
Knight's gear!**

CHAPTER FIVE

Navy Traditions

Navy Midshipmen march onto the field before the Army-Navy game, too. They wear dark-blue coats and clean white hats.

A mascot helps them cheer. "Bill the Goat" has been part of Navy tradition since 1893. Some Middies work as goat keepers to help Bill stay healthy. They also protect Bill. Army Cadets have "goat-napped" the mascot several times!

> ### HONOR
> After each Army-Navy game, the schools remember fallen heroes. In a show of sportsmanship, the students sing the official song of their opponent.

When Navy wins a game, a huge Victory Bell is rung on the **campus** in Maryland.

At every game, Midshipmen shout their biggest cheer: "Beat Army!"

◄ *For the game against Army, it's not just a few students who attend. The entire student body of the Naval Academy marches on before the game.*

CHAPTER SIX

Army Heroes

Army's greatest stars played together from 1944 to 1946. Felix "Doc" Blanchard was called "Mr. Inside." Glenn Davis had the nickname "Mr. Outside." Together, the two running backs made Army national champs.

Blanchard won the Heisman Trophy in 1945. The award goes to college football's best player. Davis won it in 1946.

Pete Dawkins was the next Heisman winner from Army. In 1958, he led the team to a No. 3 ranking.

FOOTBALL HERO

Alejandro Villanueva is an NFL star with the Pittsburgh Steelers. He played at Army. Then he served in the Army Rangers for three years. He won a Bronze Star for bravery. After his service, he started his NFL career.

Left: Glenn Davis and Felix "Doc" Blanchard

Below: Alejandro Villanueva

ARMY
AND
NAVY

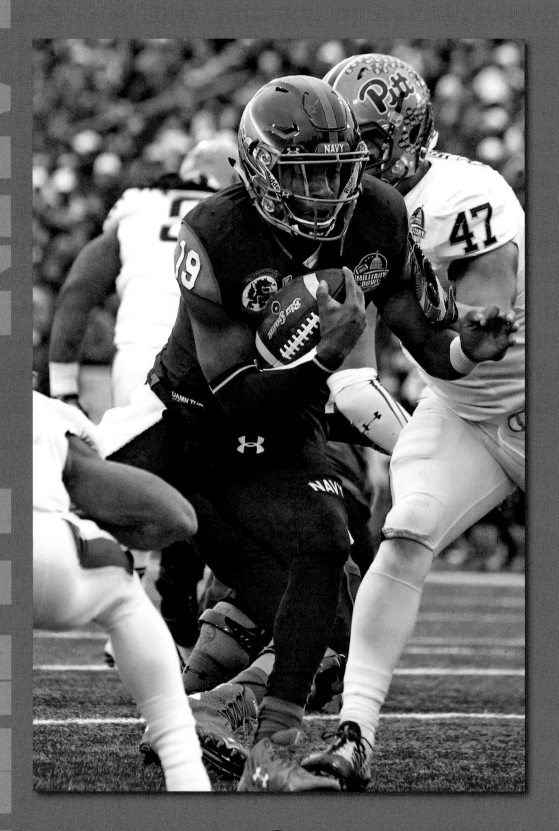

CHAPTER SEVEN

Navy Heroes

Navy has had a lot of great players. The first national star was running back Joe Bellino. He won the Heisman Trophy in 1960.

Three years later, quarterback Roger Staubach won the award. After serving in the Navy, he was a Hall of Fame QB in the NFL for the Dallas Cowboys.

As a running back, Napoleon McCallum was a two-time member of the **All-America** team (1984–85). He scored 31 touchdowns in his Navy career.

BEST RECORD

The top goal for Navy players is to beat Army. QB Keenan Reynolds beat Army four times in a row! In 2015, he led Navy to its best record ever at 11–2. He ran for 88 touchdowns. That's the most ever by a college player.

◄ *Keenan Reynolds played quarterback for Navy. Unlike most QBs, he ran on almost every play. His speed and skills made him a star.*

CHAPTER EIGHT

The Rivalry

When Army and Navy play, the game is watched all over the world. Soldiers and sailors tune in from bases and ships.

Since 1930, the game has almost always been played in Philadelphia. The city is midway between West Point and Annapolis. The US president often attends the games to cheer for both teams. The annual game is one of college football's most famous traditions.

ONE MORE RIVAL

The U.S. Air Force Academy also has a football team. The Falcons play Army and Navy each year, too. The team with the best record in those games wins the Commander-in-Chief's Trophy. The award is named for the president.

Through 2020, Navy led the all-time series. Their record was 61 wins, 53 losses, and seven ties.

Students from both schools are studying to serve their country. The American flag is flown throughout the stadium. ➤

GLOSSARY

All-America (ALL uh-MAYR-ih-kuh) an honor given to the top players in college sports

bowl games (BOWLE GAYMS) contests held after college football's regular season to which only the best teams are invited

campus (KAM-puss) the grounds and buildings of a school

capped off (KAPT OFF) finished

decades (DEK-ayds) periods of ten years

mascot (MASS-kot) a symbol of a school or a sports team, ususally an animal

rivalry (RY-vul-ree) a series of games played between the same two teams year after year

winning records (WIN-ing REK-urdz) describing a season in which a team won more games than it lost

IN THE LIBRARY

Feinstein, John. *The Rivalry: Mystery at the Army-Navy Game*. New York, NY: Yearling, 2011.

Jacobs, Greg. *The Everything Kids' Football Book*. Avon, MA: Adams Media, 2018.

Sports Illustrated Kids editors. *The Greatest Football Teams of All Time*. New York, NY: Sports Illustrated Kids, 2018.

ON THE WEB

Visit our website for links about
Army and Navy football:
childsworld.com/links

INDEX

ABOUT THE AUTHOR

K.C. Kelley is the author of more than
100 sports books for young readers, including
numerous biographies of famous athletes. He went
to the University of California—Berkeley, but his
Golden Bears didn't quite make it into this series!